My Best Book of Mummies

Philip Steele

932

KINGfISHER

Author: Philip Steele
Consultant: Dr Anne Millard
Managing Editor: Camilla Hallinan
Series Editor: Sue Nicholson
Illustrators: Vanessa Card, Angus
  McBride, Nicki Palin, Mark Peppe
Art Editor: Christina Fraser
Art Director and cover design:
  Terry Woodley
Series Designer: Ben White

Production Controller: Kelly Johnson
Printed in Hong Kong

KINGFISHER
An imprint of Kingfisher Publications Plc
New Penderel House,
283–288 High Holborn,
London WC1V 7HZ

First published by Kingfisher Publications Plc 1998

10 9 8 7 6 5 4 3 2 1

Copyright © Kingfisher Publications Plc 1998

A CIP catalogue record for this book is
available from the British Library.

ISBN 0 7534 0215 7

Contents

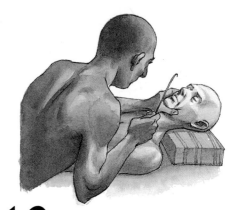

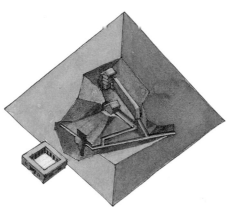

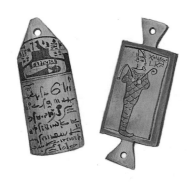

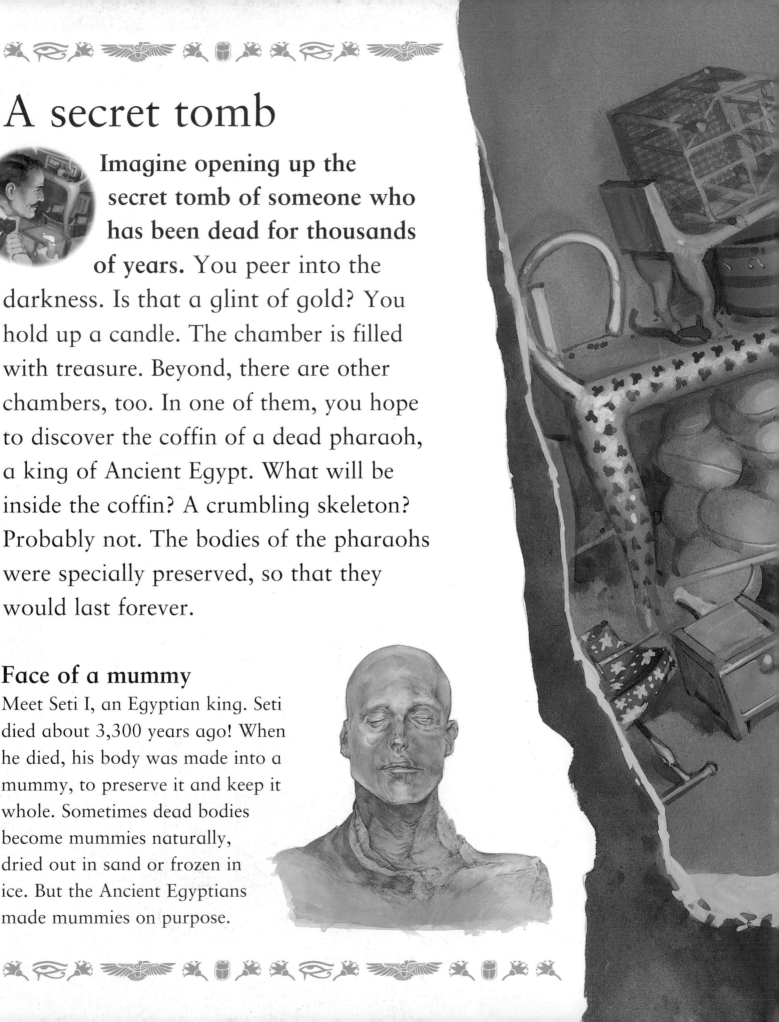

A secret tomb

Imagine opening up the secret tomb of someone who has been dead for thousands of years. You peer into the darkness. Is that a glint of gold? You hold up a candle. The chamber is filled with treasure. Beyond, there are other chambers, too. In one of them, you hope to discover the coffin of a dead pharaoh, a king of Ancient Egypt. What will be inside the coffin? A crumbling skeleton? Probably not. The bodies of the pharaohs were specially preserved, so that they would last forever.

Face of a mummy

Meet Seti I, an Egyptian king. Seti died about 3,300 years ago! When he died, his body was made into a mummy, to preserve it and keep it whole. Sometimes dead bodies become mummies naturally, dried out in sand or frozen in ice. But the Ancient Egyptians made mummies on purpose.

The pharaohs

Why did the Ancient Egyptians turn bodies into mummies? They believed a dead person needed his or her body to enjoy life in the Next World. It was particularly important for the pharaohs to be made into mummies. The pharaohs were powerful kings who ruled Egypt for thousands of years. The Ancient Egyptians believed that the pharaohs were living gods. If the magical link between the pharaohs and the Next World were broken, then the whole earth would vanish into darkness and chaos.

Gifts for a living god

The pharaoh and his queen received all kinds of gifts from people of other lands – ivory elephant tusks, animal skins, spices, gold and jewels. Riches like these were placed in the pharaoh's tomb so that he could use them when he reached the Next World.

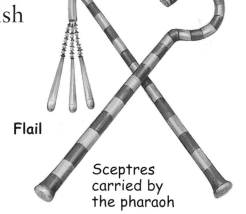

Crook

Flail

Sceptres carried by the pharaoh

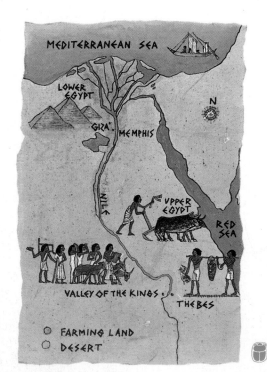

The land of Egypt

The pharaohs ruled over the green lands around the River Nile and the dusty deserts beyond. They built great cities, tombs and temples.

The Egyptian people

People believed that the pharaoh protected Egypt from disaster, but really it was the hard work of thousands of ordinary people that kept the kingdom going.

The pharaoh was at the head of Egyptian society. Beneath him were other members of the royal family. Below them were the nobles, followed by the wealthy middle classes. At the bottom were the peasants who farmed the land. Normally only rich people could afford to have their bodies turned into mummies.

Top people

The royal family lived in palaces, ate fine food and enjoyed hunting and music. Some nobles became royal officials, such as governors. Others were generals or priests.

Hard workers

Most Egyptians had to work hard. Farmers planted crops and looked after cattle. They also had to help in the building of huge temples or tombs.

Slaves were usually foreign prisoners of war. They were often used to do dangerous jobs, such as mining.

Peasants, unskilled workers, slaves

Pharaoh, queen, the royal family

In the middle

Engineers, architects, doctors and skilled craftworkers were well respected and often rich. So were the government officials, clerks and writers known as scribes.

Nobles, governors, generals, chief priests

Scribes, doctors, engineers, merchants, top craftworkers

Professional mourners, minor priests and priestesses, craftworkers

Soldiers, sailors, household servants, performers, dancers

9

Gods and goddesses

The Ancient Egyptians worshipped hundreds of gods and goddesses.

Nut and **Geb**
Sky goddess (covered in stars) and god of the Earth

Ra (or **Re**)
God of the Sun

Osiris
God of death and rebirth

Isis
Mother goddess, wife of Osiris

Anubis
God of burial and mummy-makers

River

Atum

Hathor

Ferryman

The Next World

The Ancient Egyptians believed that when they died they would travel to the Next World, the Kingdom of Osiris. They believed this kingdom was a wonderful place, and that whoever managed to reach it would live forever. However, the journey to the Next World was long and hard. On the journey, the dead needed food and drink. Their bodies had to be whole and strong. And the priests had to chant spells to protect them.

Seth
God of chaos
and confusion

Horus
Sky god, protector
of pharaohs

Amun
Creator god and
god of Thebes

Hathor
Goddess of
love and beauty

Thoth
God of writing
and knowledge

Judges   Weighing of the heart   Kingdom of Osiris

A difficult journey

The dead person asks a ferryman to help him cross a river into the Next World. Then he must pass through seven closely guarded gates.

He must fight snakes and crocodiles, and evil gods try to trap him in a net. But he also gets help from the god Atum and food and water from Hathor. He must then face 42 judges before his heart is weighed against the feather of truth. If his heart is heavy with sin, he will be gobbled up by a monster. If it is light, he will be saved.

Making a mummy

Welcome to the necropolis, the city of the dead! Here, the people who turned dead bodies into mummies worked. The skills of embalming, or mummy-making, were passed on from father to son. Embalmers learned how to remove a body's insides, dry it with salty crystals, then bandage it from head to toe. As they worked, a priest chanted prayers, or spells, from the Book of the Dead, to protect the dead person on his or her journey to the Next World.

Book of the Dead
The Book of the Dead contained over 200 spells in Egyptian picture-writing, called hieroglyphs.

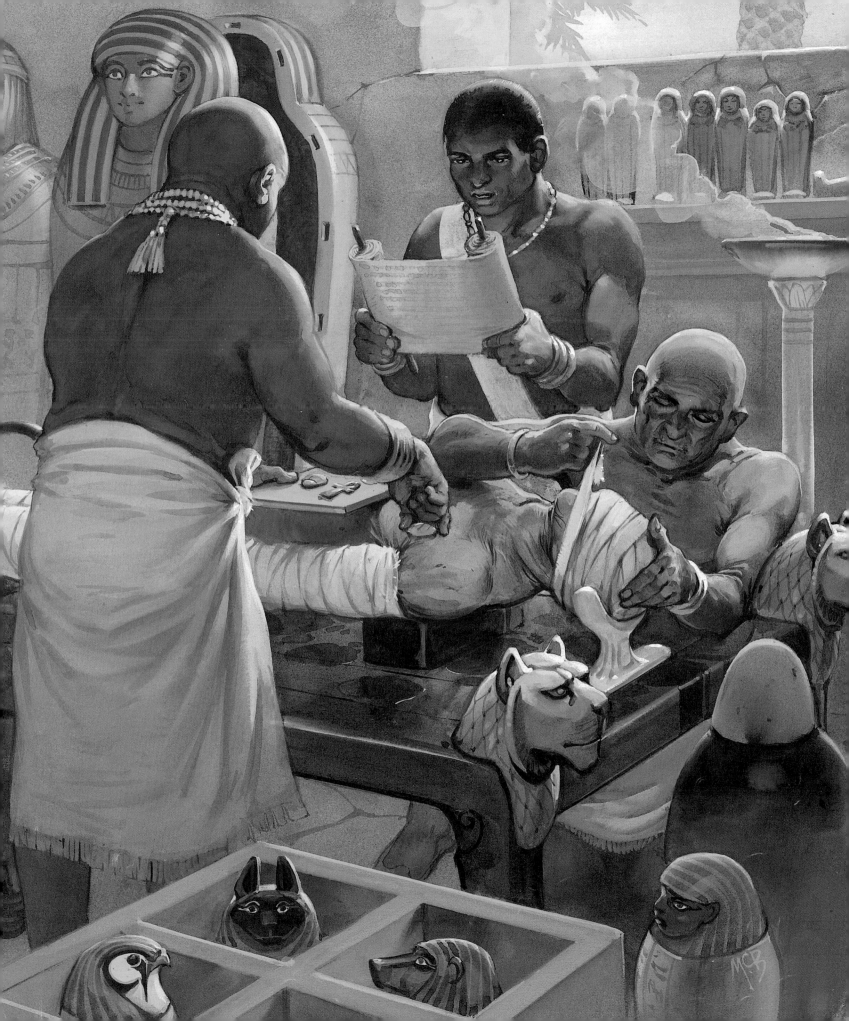

A grisly job

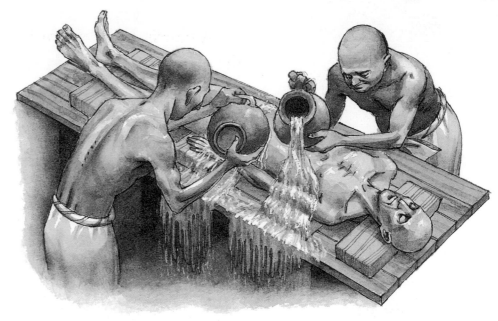

▶ First, the embalmers washed the dead person's body with water or sweet-smelling palm oil.

▼ The brain was pulled out through the nose, bit by bit, using a long bronze hook.

▶ The heart was left in the body, but the intestines, liver, lungs and stomach were cut out. They were dried in a kind of salt, called natron. Then they were covered with gum taken from trees, bandaged, and placed in special jars.

Priest wearing mask of jackal-headed god, Anubis

◀ The body was put in a bath of natron to dry it. After 40 days, it was taken out. Its insides were stuffed with linen cloth, sand or sawdust. Sometimes, the bandaged intestines, liver, stomach and lungs were put back inside.

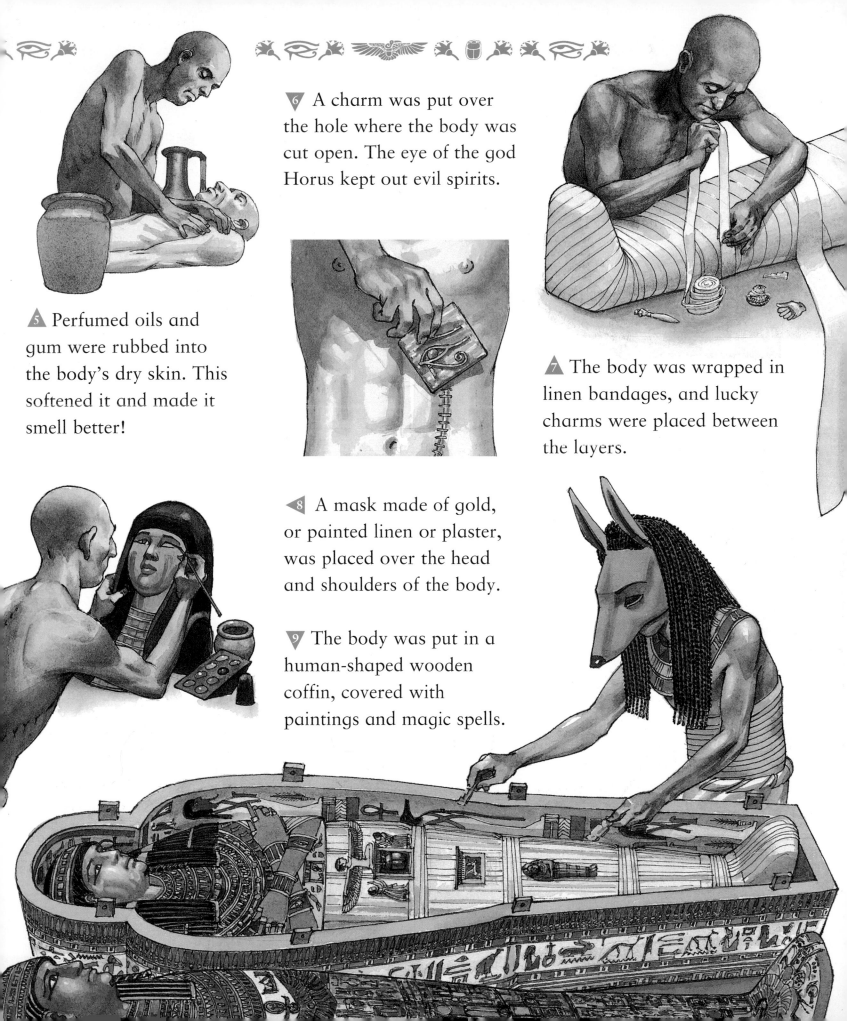

6 A charm was put over the hole where the body was cut open. The eye of the god Horus kept out evil spirits.

5 Perfumed oils and gum were rubbed into the body's dry skin. This softened it and made it smell better!

7 The body was wrapped in linen bandages, and lucky charms were placed between the layers.

8 A mask made of gold, or painted linen or plaster, was placed over the head and shoulders of the body.

9 The body was put in a human-shaped wooden coffin, covered with paintings and magic spells.

Canopic jars

The preserved liver, lungs, stomach and intestines were usually stored in jars, called canopic jars. The jars were put in a box, then placed in the mummy's tomb. Each jar had a stopper in the shape of a head. Sometimes these were all human heads. More often, they showed human, jackal, baboon and falcon heads.

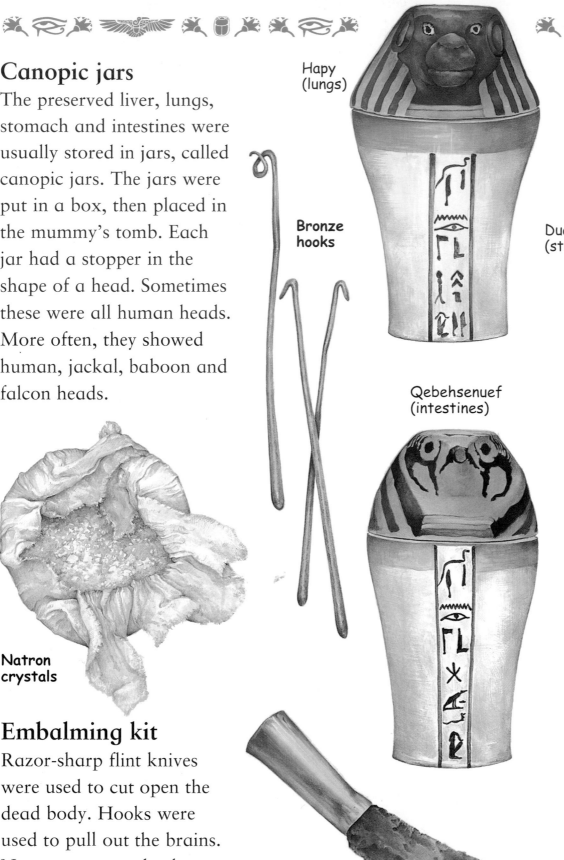

Hapy (lungs)

Bronze hooks

Qebehsenuef (intestines)

Natron crystals

Embalming kit

Razor-sharp flint knives were used to cut open the dead body. Hooks were used to pull out the brains. Natron, a natural salt, was used to dry it out.

Flint knife

Canopic jars with the heads of the four sons of the god Horus

Duamutef (stomach)

Imsety (liver)

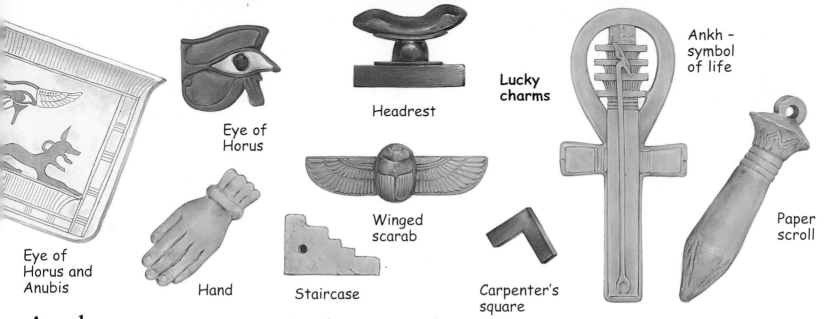

Eye of Horus and Anubis

Eye of Horus

Hand

Headrest

Staircase

Winged scarab

Carpenter's square

Lucky charms

Ankh – symbol of life

Paper scroll

Amulets

Magic charms, or amulets, were often placed in the mummy's bandages.

Amulets were made of gold, stone, clay or wax. They came in many shapes and sizes.

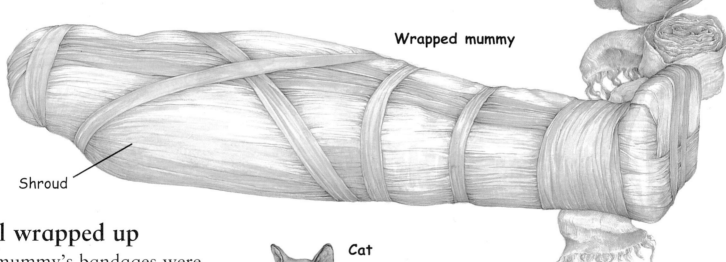

Bandages

Wrapped mummy

Shroud

All wrapped up

A mummy's bandages were made of linen, never wool. The holiest bandages came from clothes that had been placed on the statues of gods in temples. The final layer was often a large sheet, or a shroud. Bandaging a mummy took 15 days.

Cat

Dog

Animal mummies

The Egyptians believed that many animals were holy or sacred. These animals were often made into mummies, just like humans. So were favourite family pets.

A funeral procession

A funeral procession is winding its way from the city of Thebes along the banks of the River Nile. Slowly, it climbs towards the edge of the desert, where a tomb has been carved in the rocky cliffs. Oxen haul the coffin over the stony ground on a boat-shaped sledge. Meanwhile, priests sprinkle milk and burn sweet-smelling incense. Women weep and wail as the procession passes by.

Opening of the mouth

At a special ceremony, the priests "opened the mouth" of the mummy so that the dead person could speak and move in the Next World.

Funeral boats

Sometimes, mummies were carried on models of boats or shown on a boat in a painting in their tomb. This was a symbol of the journey by water to meet Osiris.

Funeral
pit
5,200
years ago

Coffins and cases

In the early days of Ancient Egypt, people were buried in pits in the desert. The hot sand soon dried out their bodies naturally. Later, the Egyptians buried bodies in simple reed and wooden coffins, but these bodies soon turned into skeletons. From about 4,600 years ago, the Egyptians began to embalm bodies. Embalming continued for nearly 3,000 years.

Reed
coffin
5,100
years ago

Wooden coffin
4,020 years
ago

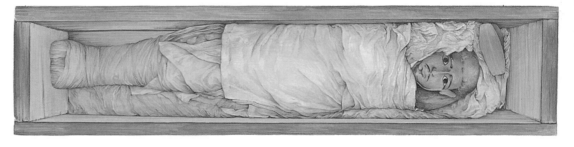

Mummy cases

Later, mummies were put into human-shaped coffins, or cases. The golden coffin below was made for a priestess from Thebes. Mummy cases were often covered in magic spells to keep the mummy safe.

3,650
years ago

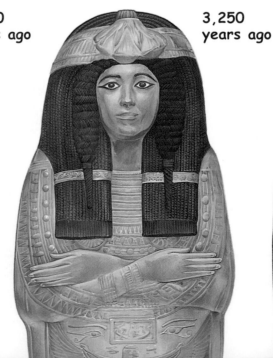

3,250
years ago

2,650
years a

Nest of coffins

The body of the pharaoh Tutankhamun was protected by a nest of human-shaped mummy cases. The cases were put inside a big stone box called a sarcophagus. Each mummy case was decorated with gold and jewels. The mummy itself was wearing a beautiful mask made from solid gold.

The coffins all provided a home for Tutankhamun's spirit, or ka.

When the Romans ruled Egypt, the paintings on coffins were more realistic.

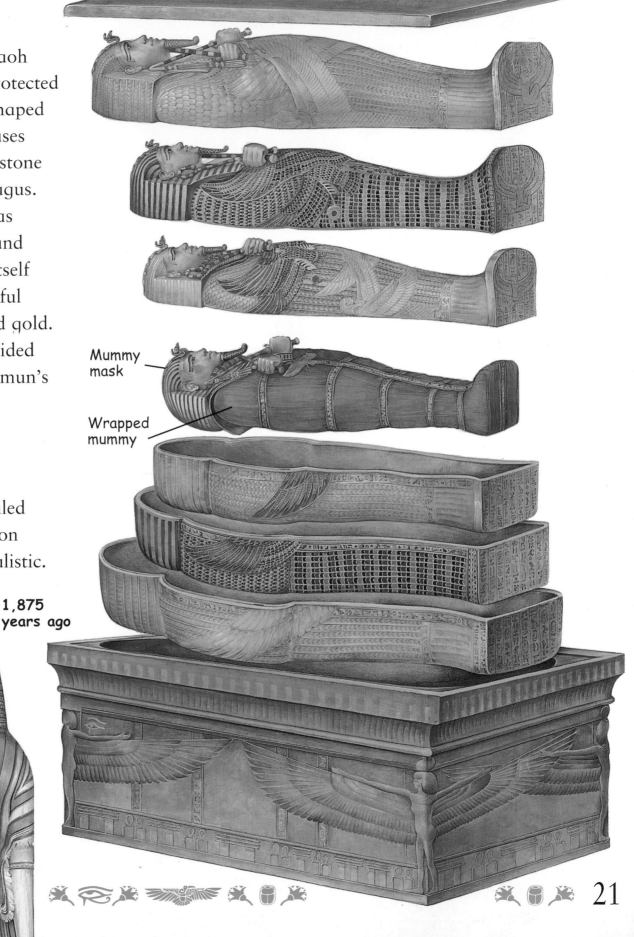

Mummy mask

Wrapped mummy

1,875 years ago

Food for the dead

Food and drink were left in tombs for the ka, or spirit, of the dead person. People believed that the ka needed these for nourishment. In the tomb of the young pharaoh Tutankhamun, archaeologists found 116 baskets of fruit and 40 jars of wine as well as boxes of roast meat and bread.

Duck

Goose

Wine

Rush container

Figs

Bread

Model servants

Little statues were often placed in tombs, too. A spell would make them come alive so that they could work for the dead person in the Next World. Some figures looked life-like. Others were shaped like tiny mummies and were called shabtis.

Sailing boat

Lady's maid

Threshing

Ploughing

Mummy-shaped shabti figures

Fine furniture

Tombs also contained many beautiful pieces of furniture, such as beds, stools and thrones made of cedar wood, ebony, ivory and gold.

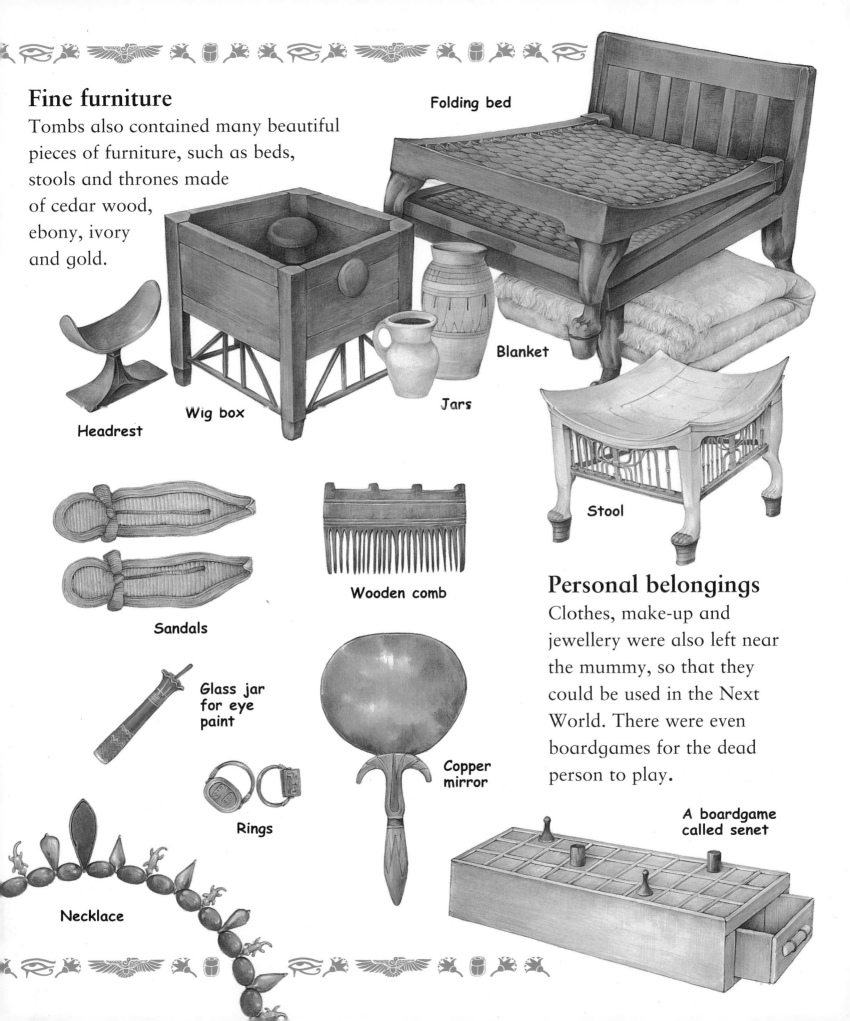

Folding bed

Blanket

Jars

Wig box

Headrest

Stool

Sandals

Wooden comb

Glass jar for eye paint

Rings

Copper mirror

Necklace

Personal belongings

Clothes, make-up and jewellery were also left near the mummy, so that they could be used in the Next World. There were even boardgames for the dead person to play.

A boardgame called senet

A mummy's tomb

Over thousands of years, rich Egyptians built different kinds of tombs for their mummies. Most mummies were buried in underground chambers. Some of these were carved out of solid rock. Some had a building with rooms built over the top. One room was used as a chapel for the dead.

All the tombs served the same purpose. They had to protect the remains of the dead person and his or her possessions from sandstorms, robberies and other disasters.

Offerings to the dead

Outside many tombs were special stone tables where food, drink or other offerings could be left for the mummy's ka.

A priest, or a relative of the dead person, would pray for the offerings to be accepted. The words of the prayers were carved on to stone slabs around the tomb.

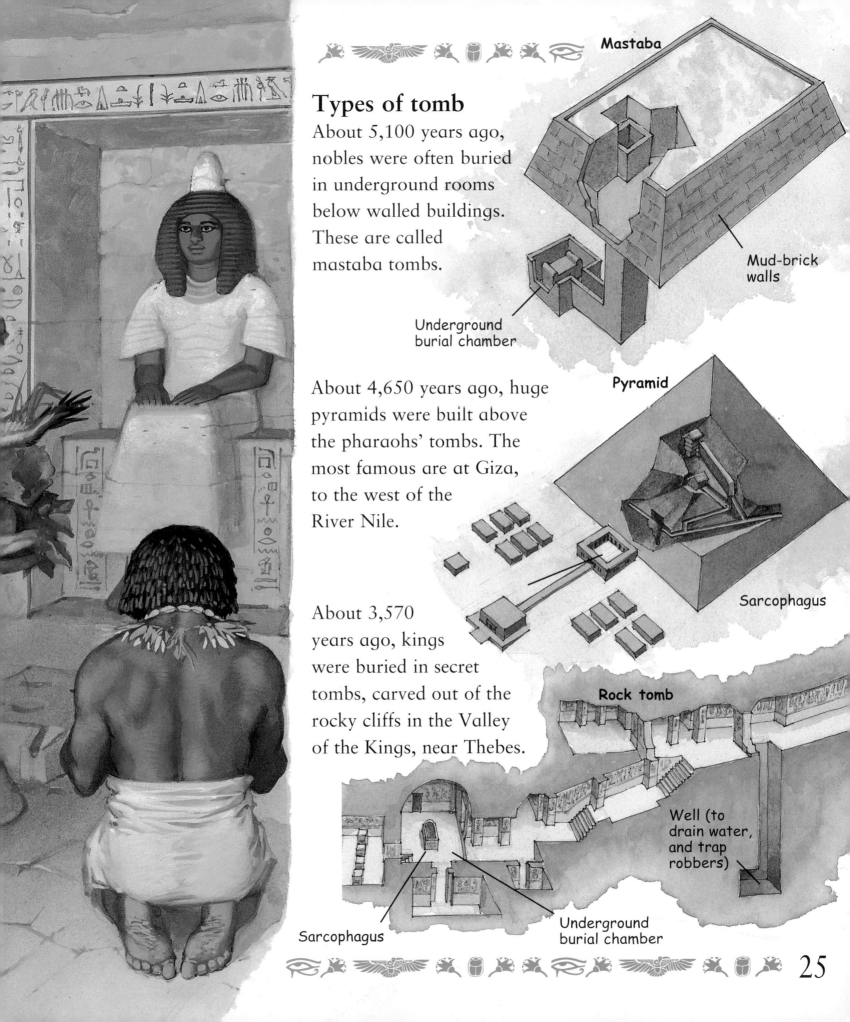

Types of tomb

About 5,100 years ago, nobles were often buried in underground rooms below walled buildings. These are called mastaba tombs.

About 4,650 years ago, huge pyramids were built above the pharaohs' tombs. The most famous are at Giza, to the west of the River Nile.

About 3,570 years ago, kings were buried in secret tombs, carved out of the rocky cliffs in the Valley of the Kings, near Thebes.

Mastaba

Mud-brick walls

Underground burial chamber

Pyramid

Sarcophagus

Rock tomb

Well (to drain water, and trap robbers)

Sarcophagus

Underground burial chamber

Robbers!

Robbers are breaking into a royal tomb in the Valley of the Kings. They have crept past the guard, and have tunnelled down to the burial chamber. They are nervous. They may still fall into one of the wells built into the tomb's passageways. And if they are caught, they will probably be killed. But if they can escape with even a tiny gold statue, they will be able to live in comfort for the rest of their lives.

Mummy magic
During the Middle Ages, people in Europe used stolen bits of mummies to make medicines.

Treasure hunters
When French soldiers invaded Egypt 200 years ago, treasure hunters dug up many mummies.

A new tomb

1 In 1908, some pots and cloth were found in the Valley of the Kings, near the ancient city of Thebes. They had been used to prepare the mummy of a pharaoh called Tutankhamun. But where was his tomb?

2 In 1922, the archaeologist Howard Carter found the entrance to the tomb. When his employer, Lord Carnarvon, arrived they broke into the first room.

3 Inside, they discovered heaps of golden treasure. It had been disturbed by robbers, but there were still over 600 items.

4 Carter was very excited at this discovery. But he and his team had to work slowly and carefully.

Every item in the chamber had to be photographed, measured and listed before it was removed.

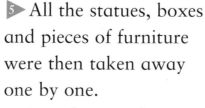

5 All the statues, boxes and pieces of furniture were then taken away one by one.

It took several years to clear the tomb.

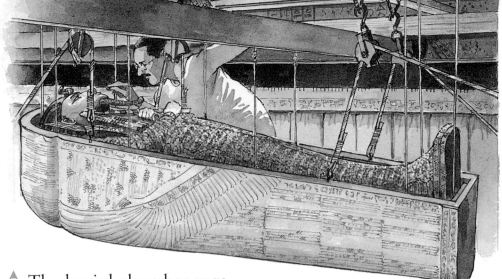

▼ Would the next room hold the 3,500-year-old mummy of Tutankhamun? The king of Egypt himself watched as Carter opened the burial chamber. Inside, they saw a wall of gold.

7 The burial chamber was closely packed with four golden shrines. Inside the shrines was a sarcophagus containing three mummy cases. The innermost one held the mummy of the pharaoh. The cases were so heavy, Carter had to use pulleys to lift them.

Plan of the tomb

Carter had two more rooms to explore. Both were full of treasure. Tutankhamun was not a famous king, but his tomb was an exciting find because his burial chamber had not been robbed.

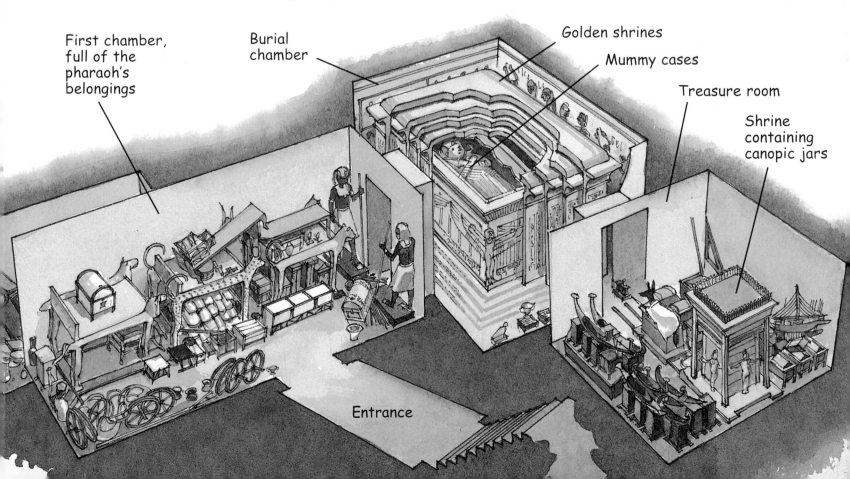

First chamber, full of the pharaoh's belongings

Burial chamber

Golden shrines

Mummy cases

Treasure room

Shrine containing canopic jars

Entrance

Mummies and science

Since the days of Howard Carter, scientists have been able to discover more and more about mummies. Today, scientists can take a small tissue sample from a mummy, such as a bit of bone or skin, and work out who its relatives were or whether it had any diseases.

Dating a mummy

Scientists can work out accurate dates from cloth and the wood in coffins and mummy tags.

Mummy tags - found on some mummies

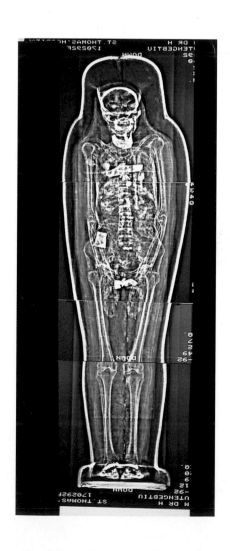

Scanning a mummy

When a hospital needs to see inside someone's body, it may use a scanner. Scanners are now used to examine mummies, too, without having to remove all their bandages.

From scans, scientists can study how the mummy was bandaged, what kind of amulets were used, and whether the mummy had any broken bones.

The last meal

Scientists can examine the stomach and intestines of a mummy to work out what it ate just before it died.

Duck

Bread

Beetles and bugs

Tiny creepy-crawlies found in a mummy's coffin tell us what kinds of insects lived in Ancient Egypt.

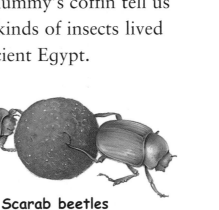

Scarab beetles

Model of a mummy

Sometimes it's hard to imagine a mummy as a living, breathing person. But experts can make a model of a mummy's head by studying its skull. For example, scientists worked out that one mummy had a broken nose because of the way the bone had healed.

Models like this show us what the person looked like thousands of years ago.

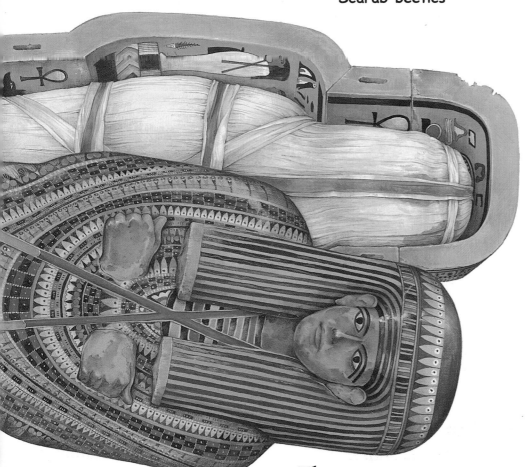

Lotus flower – often used in necklaces and wreaths

Flowers

Scientists know what time of year someone died from dried flowers in their tomb.

Glossary

amulet A charm which is believed to protect its wearer from evil.

archaeologist Someone who digs up and studies ancient ruins and remains.

Book of the Dead A group of about 200 spells to help the dead person in the Next World.

canopic jar A container that held the embalmed internal organs (stomach, liver, intestines and lungs) of a dead person. In the Middle Kingdom, the lids of the jars had human heads. By the New Kingdom, the lids were made to look like the heads of the four sons of the god Horus – man, baboon, jackal and hawk.

chamber A small room.

crook and flail Sceptres of the god Osiris. Also used by the pharaohs.

embalmer Someone who treats dead bodies so that they do not rot away.

hieroglyphs One of the ways of writing used in Ancient Egypt. Made up of tiny pictures and symbols.

jackal A wild dog found in Africa and Asia.

ka The force or spirit which the Ancient Egyptians believed lived on after the body died.

mastaba An early type of Ancient Egyptian tomb, made up of an underground chamber, buildings and a wall.

Middle Kingdom The second of three great periods of Ancient Egyptian history, from 1991 to 1786 BC. During this period, Egypt conquered Nubia, and became a stong trading power.

natron Natural mineral salt, found in old lake beds in Ancient Egypt, and used in embalming.

necropolis An area where dead bodies were embalmed and buried.

New Kingdom The third of three great periods of Ancient Egyptian history, from 1570 to 1070 BC.

During this period, the pharaohs Tutankhamun and Rameses II reigned.

Next World The place a person's spirit or soul went to after they had died.

Old Kingdom The first of three great periods of Ancient Egyptian history from 2686 to 2181 BC. The pyramids at Giza were built during this period.

Opening of the Mouth A ceremony in the Ancient Egyptian burial service. It involved touching the mummy with a special tool to open the mouth and give the power of speech and movement back to the mummy.

pharaoh A ruler of Ancient Egypt.

pyramid A large pointed or step-sided building marking the tomb of a pharaoh.

sarcophagus A large stone box in which a coffin was placed.

scarab A type of beetle, sacred to the Ancient Egyptians.

Index